Greeting Cards
made easy

Greeting Cards
made easy

Series Editors: Susan & Martin Penny

David & Charles

A DAVID & CHARLES BOOK

First published in the UK in 2000

745.5941
GREE

32530 60540 8333

A catalogue record for this book is available from the British Library.

ISBN 0 7153 1017 8

Series Editors: Susan & Martin Penny
Designed and produced by Penny & Penny
Illustrations: Fred Fieber at Red Crayola
Photography: John Gollop

Printed in France by Imprimerie Pollina S. A.
for David & Charles
Brunel House Newton Abbot Devon

Contents

Introduction to Greeting Cards

Greeting Cards Made Easy is a complete guide to the craft of making cards; find out how to use a variety of materials to make a range of imaginative and highly decorated cards. To make the cards you will need only very basic equipment; and the decoration can be as simple or as complicated as you choose to make it

Essential equipment

Below is a list of equipment needed for making cards:

- **Card or thick paper** – strong enough to stand up when decorated, but thin enough to score and fold.
- **Ruler** – to measure and to provide a straight edge for cutting.
- **Craft knife and cutting mat** – to cut a card mount neatly and accurately.
- **Sharp scissors** – to cut fabric, paper, and metal sheeting.
- **Pencil** – for drawing the shape of the card before cutting.
- **White paper** – for making a folded insert to put inside a card.
- **Double-sided tape** – for applying surface decoration or for gluing an insert in a card.

- **Tacky glue** – for applying decoration to a card, envelope or tag.
- **Glue gun** – for attaching heavier objects like jewels, tiles and beads to the front of a card, envelope or tag.

Materials for making cards

Almost any material can be used to make a card, but the important things to remember when making your selection are: the way the card will be folded; whether there will be a window opening; and the weight and size of the surface decoration. All these things will effect the balance and stability of the card, and should be considered when choosing the material to be used.

- **Thin card**
  This is the most useful material for making cards. It comes in a wide range of colours and weights, and can be used for single or double folded cards with three panels, both with or without a window opening.
- **Thick paper**
  This can be used in the same way as the thin card, but it may need to be folded in half and then half again to make a double layered, single folded card.
- **Thick watercolour paper**
  Strong but very thick, so use as a single folded card, with or without a window opening.
- **Thick handmade paper**
  Use it to make a single folded card, with torn edges.
- **Corrugated card**
  This is not the same product that is used to wrap parcels, but a stronger coloured version of the card available from craft shops. Use it for a single folded card, without a window.

Tips for making cards

- Measure and cut the rectangle of paper to be used for the card very accurately, making sure the corners are exact 90° angles
- Use the back (blunt side) of a craft knife to score the fold lines
- Make sure you enlarge or reduce all the tracings for each project in this book by the same percentage
- Use a ball-point pen to draw design lines on to foam sheet, and always cut using a craft knife and cutting mat
- Use scissors to cut metal sheeting
- Punch holes in metal sheeting using a punching tool, on a soft wooden board with a rubber mallet
- Patterns can be embossed on to the back of metal sheeting using a blunt pencil or an empty ballpoint pen
- When using a ruler to draw lines with a metallic pen, turn it on to its convex side as this will stop the ink from spreading
- Wet the edges of handmade paper before tearing
- Odd earrings or a backless brooch can be used to decorate cards
- Use blu-tack to temporarily attach a bead, stone or other heavy object to the front of a card to check the balance, and if necessary adjust the weight of the paper used for the card
- Always use flexible glass paint in a tube when working on acetate, then when the paint is dry and the acetate bends, the paint will not peel off the acetate
- Use deckle-edged scissors to give card edges a decorative finish
- Hang a mobile behind a window opening using invisible embroidery thread
- Use a glue gun to attach heavy decorative objects to cards and tags

Adding decoration

Here are just a few of the items that can be used to decorate cards

- Foam sheet, cork
- Metal sheeting, metal cut from pet food tins
- Fabric, ribbon, lace, hessian
- Jewels, mirrors and old jewellery
- Shells, stones, beads
- Buttons, mosaic tiles
- Dried flowers, bark, twigs, leaves, raffia
- Pom poms, chenille sticks, toy eyes
- Psychedelic paper, handmade paper
- Cake decorating, silk or paper flowers
- Outliner paste, glass paint
- Metallic pens, glitter glue, watercolour pencils
- Corrugated card, metallic card

Card accessories

- **Envelopes** – use thick paper in a colour which tones with the card, adding decoration to the front and back flap.

- **Tags** – use the same materials as the card, and a small part of the card design.
- **Presentation box** – if the card is heavy, or has a lot of surface decoration, the only way to send it may be in a presentation box. Cover a recycled box with toning paper and then decorate to match the card.
- **Gift bag** – Make a gift or party bag using matching paper, and then add decoration to match the card.

Making a Card Mount

You need no special equipment to make professional looking card mounts at home, just a pencil, sharp craft knife, a straight edge and a cutting mat or board. The card you choose needs to be thick enough to stand up when decorated, but thin enough to fold on the score. Accurate cutting and folding will ensure a good finish

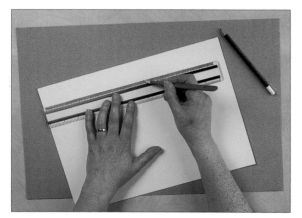

1 Using a pencil, straight edge and craft knife, mark and then cut a rectangle from thin card. The corners must be exact right angles or the edges will not come together when folded. The size of the rectangle should be the height of your card and twice its width.

3 With the scored line on the outside, the card will now bend easily in half. Do not put too much pressure on the fold until the card edges have been lined up. Press along the score, and then sharpen the fold with your thumb or a small craft roller.

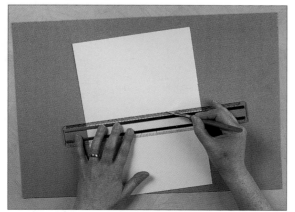

2 Draw a fine pencil line across the middle front of the card. Score the line using the back of the craft knife blade. This will make a sharp indentation but will not cut the card.

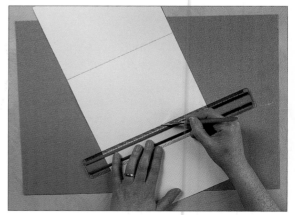

4 A double folded card has three panels and two scores. Divide the card into three, making one of the outer panels 1mm ($^1/_{16}$in) smaller than the other. Score and fold twice.

Handmade paper card

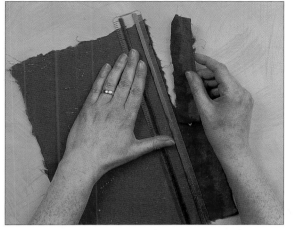

1 Handmade paper can be used to make cards, as long as it is thick enough to stay in shape when decorated; but not so thick that it is difficult to cut or fold. The edges of the paper can be cut using scissors; for a rougher, natural look, draw a faint pencil line, wet the paper, and then tear slowly, working against a ruler. This will give an uneven, torn finish to the edge of the card.

2 Score the paper down through the middle using a ruler and the back of a craft knife. With the scored line on the outside, bend the card in half, then press along the score. If you are using dark coloured paper, use double-sided tape to stick a folded, white paper insert inside the card on which to write your message.

Cutting an aperture

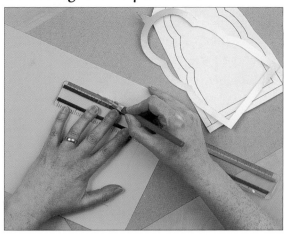

Use a pencil and ruler to mark a window opening on the front flap of your card. Take great care that the window is central, and that all the corners are 90° angles. Cut out the window using a craft knife. For a double folded card with three panels, the window must be in the middle panel.

Adding a decorative panel

An extra layer or panel can be added to the front of a dark or plain card as a base for the decoration. Cut the panel from textured or plain paper or card, fabric, or wide ribbon. Finish the edges of the panel with torn, frayed or decorated edges using deckle-edged scissors. Glue the panel to the card front.

Finishing Techniques

Handmade paper, tin, foam and acetate are just a few of the materials that can be used to decorate cards. When adding 3-D embellishment to the front of a card, remember to get the correct balance or the card will not stand up. If the card is an unusual shape or size you may need to make a special envelope or presentation box

Cutting and painting foam

1 Mark the design directly on to the surface of the foam using a fine marker pen; or make a paper template of the design and draw around it. Lay the foam on to a cutting mat and cut around the design lines using a sharp craft knife.

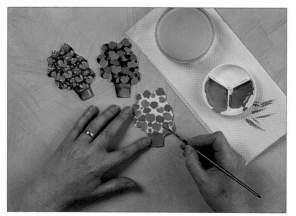

2 Using a small brush, build up the design using several thin layers of acrylic paint. The design can be painted freehand or marked on to the foam using a marker pen.

Cutting and punching tin

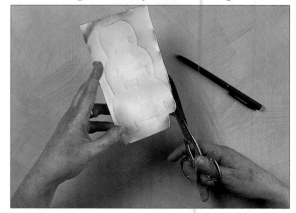

1 Transfer the design on to tin sheeting using a ball-point pen. Cut around the outer edge of the design using a large pair of scissors. For the smaller cut-away areas use small scissors or a craft knife. Take care not to cut your hands on the sharp metal edges.

2 Place the metal on to a soft wooden board. Place the tip of the punching tool on the metal and gently hit the tool with the hammer, making a hole in the metal.

Using artificial flowers

Flowers used for decorating cakes, or small silk or paper flowers which are very lightweight all make good card decorations. The flowers and leaves can be glued individually on to the front of the card, or attached in small bunches, held together with florist's wire, then wrapped in cellophane and ribbon.

Using dried flowers

Small dried flowers, seed heads and lavender can be used to decorate cards. Use flowers that are the correct proportion for the card, cutting them individually from the bunches. Leave a small length of stem on each flower; if a stem is weak or broken, strengthen it with a piece of fine wire.

Using outliner paste

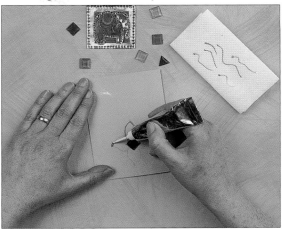

Outliner paste can be used on almost any surface to add detail, or to outline objects like jewels, fabric or metal sheeting. Squeeze the tube of outliner paste gently, as if using an icing tube. The spread of the paste will depend on the temperature: warm, dry conditions are best.

Using buttons and beads

Small jewels, beads, buttons, mosaic tiles and old jewellery – a single earring or a backless brooch can be used to decorate cards, as long as they have one flat side. Glue a piece of torn handmade paper, card, or fabric on to the card and then mount the object using tacky glue or a glue gun.

Painting acetate

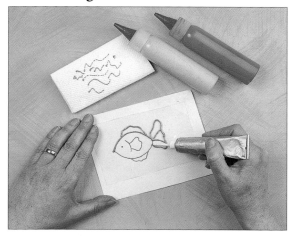

1 Use thick acetate to make a window in a card, or to make a hanging mobile. Use outliner paste to draw the shape on to the surface of the acetate, making sure there are no gaps in the paste, especially at the intersections. Use flexible glass paint in a squeezable tube, which should be applied directly on to the surface of the acetate. Use a cocktail stick to blend the colours together.

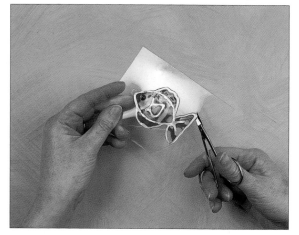

2 Once the paint is dry, cut out the shape just outside the outer paste line. Suspend the painted shape on invisible thread in the window opening of the card. If the acetate has to fit exactly into an opening cut in the card, make it slightly bigger, and then glue it behind the opening, inside the card.

Using glitter glue

Glitter glue is very easy to use on cards, and comes in gold, silver, and a range of bright colours. Shake the tube before you begin, then squeeze it gently on to the card. Use it freehand, against a straight edge, or over a pencil line drawn on the card. Leave the glitter glue to dry overnight.

Drawing an outline

A metallic pen can be used to outline a window opening, or to add a border around the outside of the card. Choose a pen with a fine nib; shake the pen well, and then make straight, dotted or dashed lines on the card. Work freehand, over a pencil line, or against a ruler or straight edge.

Making Card Accessories

To make a handmade card into an extra special gift, add a matching tag and decorated envelope. Finish the tag in the same material and colour as the card; the envelope can be decorated with a metallic pen and outliner paste, with a smaller version of the card design attached to the front or the back flap

Making gift tags

1 Cut a tag from the same paper as you are using for the card. Choose an area of the card design that fits on to the tag; or use a larger part, make a tracing, and then reduce its size on a photocopier. Punch one or two holes on one side of the tag.

2 Decorate the tag using the same materials as the card. Thread the tag with a length of raffia, string, thread or ribbon, then finish the ends with a bow or knot.

Making an envelope

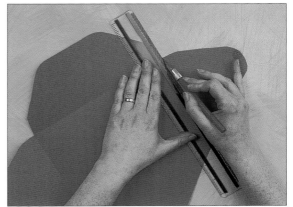

1 Lay the card down on to thick, coloured paper. Draw a rectangle on to the paper, using a pencil and ruler, slightly larger than the card, then add flaps to the four edges. Score along each side of the rectangle using a ruler and the back of a craft knife.

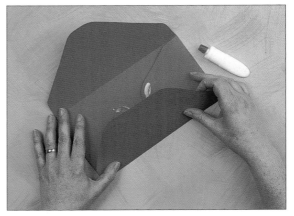

2 Fold the side flaps in, and the bottom flap up, and glue the three flaps together using tacky glue. The envelope can now be decorated to match the card.

Undersea World Cards

The watery scenes on these cards, envelopes and tags have been painted on to acetate using flexible glass paint. To give a three dimensional effect, some of the fish have been suspended on invisible thread. As they move, and the light catches their painted bodies, the fish look as if they are swimming under the deep blue sea

You will need

- Thick watercolour paper – white
- Thick acetate sheet
- Card – blue, green, purple
- Flexible glass paint in a squeezable tube that is recommended for use on acetate – gold, raspberry, light blue, dark blue, aqua, peach, orange, emerald, purple, teal, pearl white
- Outliner paste – pewter, silver
- Cocktail sticks, cotton buds
- Invisible embroidery thread
- Scissors, craft knife, cutting mat
- Pencil, ruler, masking tape, sticky tape
- Tacky glue

Making the shell card

1 Use a craft knife and cutting mat to cut a rectangle 22.5x48.6cm (8³⁄₄x19¹⁄₄in) from thick watercolour paper to make a double folded card. Divide the card into three, making the right hand outer panel 1mm (¹⁄₁₆in) smaller than the other two. Score and fold twice.

2 In the middle section of the card, draw a rectangle with a wavy edge at the top and sides, 3.5cm (1³⁄₈in) in from the edges. Open out the card then cut out the rectangle and discard the cut-out piece. Fold in the slightly smaller, right hand section of the card. Draw inside the rectangle with a pencil, on to the folded flap below. Cut the rectangle and discard. You should now have two flaps with identical rectangles cut from the centre.

3 Place a sheet of acetate over the shell card design on page 18. Use pewter outliner paste to draw around the shells, and silver for the fish. Squeeze the tube of outliner paste gently, keeping your hand steady, as if using an icing tube. All the paste lines must join together at the intersections. Use a cocktail stick to even out any blobs of paste. Leave the paste to dry.

4 To paint between the outliner paste, choose flexible glass paint that can be squeezed directly from the bottle, and is recommended

for use on acetate. Apply the paint colours next to one another, directly on to the acetate. Use a cocktail stick to drag and blend the paint colours together where they meet. Use a cotton bud to clean up any mistakes. The paint is opaque when wet but translucent when dry. Use a combination of yellow, orange and raspberry for the shells and fish, and blue for the sea. Use white to highlight the edges of the shells, and the top of the sea. Leave to dry.

5 Use scissors to cut out the shell design. Glue it to the front middle section of the card, over the bottom edge of the window opening. Cut out the three fish and suspend them on invisible thread from inside the card using sticky tape. Fold in the right hand flap of the card and glue it in place, sandwiching the thread ends between the card.

6 Finish the card by outlining the edges of the window opening on the front of the card with silver outliner paste, then add swirls and dots around the card border.

Making the envelope and tag

1 Using the design for the envelope on page 63 as a guide, draw a rectangle on bright blue card, slightly larger than your card. Add flaps to the rectangle to make an envelope shape. Cut out the envelope, then score and fold on the dotted lines. Fold the side flaps in, and the bottom up, and glue together. Paint the shell envelope design on page 17 on to acetate, in the same way as for the card. When dry, cut out and glue the shells to the front of the envelope.

2 Use a craft knife and cutting mat to cut a rectangle 7.5x8.5cm (3x3³⁄₄in) from thick watercolour paper. Cut out a rectangle from the middle of the tag, 1.5cm (⁵⁄₈in) in from the edges. Paint the single shell tag design, on

page 19, on to acetate. Once dry, cut the acetate into a rectangle, slightly larger than the hole in the tag. Glue the acetate on to the back of the tag. Decorate the tag with silver outliner paste. Punch a hole in the corner of the tag and thread with red raffia.

Making the fish scene card

1 Use a craft knife and cutting mat to cut a rectangle 22.5x48.6cm (8³⁄₄x19¹⁄₄in) from thick watercolour paper. Divide the card into three, score and fold twice in the same way as for the shell card.

2 Cut identical straight sided rectangles 3.5cm (1³⁄₈in) in from the edges, in the middle and right hand flap of the card.

3 Place acetate over the fish scene card design on page 18. Use pewter outliner paste to outline the largest fish, seaweed and rocks. Outline the small fish, frame, and bubbles using silver outliner paste. Leave to dry.

4 Paint the fish using yellow, orange, raspberry and blue glass paint; use emerald for the seaweed and dark blue for the frame. Use white for the bubbles, and to highlight the large fish, especially on the fins. Paint the three small fish in the same way, but do not

paint the area around the small fish, as this will be cut away to form a window in the acetate. Leave to dry.

5 Cut out the complete fish scene, then remove the window opening containing the small fish. Cut out the three fish. Glue the fish scene on to the front of the card, so that the acetate painted border covers the top and left hand edge of the window opening. Suspend the three small fish on invisible embroidery thread from inside the card using sticky tape. Fold in the right hand flap of the card and glue it in place, sandwiching the ends of the invisible thread securely between the card layers.

6 Finish the card by adding swirls of silver outliner paste to the edges of the card.

Making the envelope and tag

1 Make an envelope in the same way as for the shell card using bright green card. Decorate the envelope with two acetate painted fish using the design on page 19, using swirls of silver outliner paste. Make a tag in the same way as for the shell card, using the stacked fish design on page 19.

Making the fish shoal card

1 Make a double folded card in the same way as for the shell and the fish scene cards. Cut out a 18x12cm (7x4¾in) rectangular window opening from the middle and right hand flap of the card.

2 Place acetate over the shoal of fish design on page 18 and transfer the outlines to the acetate using silver outliner paste. Leave to dry. Paint the fish using aqua, emerald, teal, purple and white; a marbled mix of blues and white for the sea; and use emerald and aqua for the border. Leave to dry. Cut out the painted rectangle of swimming fish, slightly larger

than the window opening, and glue inside the card behind the window. Fold in the right hand flap, and glue the card together.

Making the envelope and tag

1 Make an envelope from purple card, then decorate it with a shoal of fish painted on to acetate using the design on this page. Add dots of silver outliner paste to the envelope, around the painted acetate panel. Make a tag with a painted acetate rectangle in the same way as for the fish and shell designs, using the shoal of fish design on page 19. Add dots of silver outliner paste around the acetate panel on the tag.

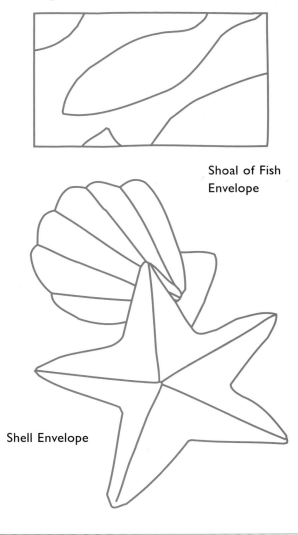

Shoal of Fish
Envelope

Shell Envelope

Shell Card

Shoal of
Fish Card

Shell Tag

Fish Scene Card

Fish Scene Envelope

Shoal of
Fish Tag

Fish
Scene
Tag

19

Bright Daisy Cards

These bright, cheery, all occasion cards are fun and easy to make. The pots of flowers have been cut from thin foam sheeting, which has then been mounted on to coloured corrugated card. Deckle-edged scissors used on the edges of the foam and card give the cards a very professional finish

You will need

- Corrugated card – red, yellow, purple
- Paper – pink, red
- Thin foam sheeting – yellow, pink, purple, blue, red, orange
- Deckle-edged scissors
- Ribbon – blue, green
- Hole punch
- Craft knife, cutting mat, scissors
- Ruler, ballpoint pen, white paper
- Tacky glue, spray adhesive

Making the tall card

1 Cut a rectangle of yellow corrugated card 21x20cm (8¼x8in) using a craft knife and cutting mat: the corrugations should run parallel with the long edge.

2 Using a straight edge and the back of a craft knife blade, make a score line midway across the width of the card, using one of the corrugations as a guide. Fold the card in half on the score line, lining up the edges of the card.

3 Cut a rectangle of pink paper 7.5x17cm (3x6¾in) and then decorate the edges using a pair of deckle-edged scissors. Glue the rectangle of paper centrally on to the front of the card using spray adhesive.

4 Make individual tracings of the different pieces that make up the large flower pot on page 23: the pot, diamond decoration, stem, flower and flower centre. Cut out each traced component from white paper.

5 Lay the traced flower on to thin purple foam, and draw round the edge using a ballpoint pen. Cut out the foam flower using a craft knife and cutting mat. Now cut the other shapes from foam: use green for the stem; blue for the vase; and red for the flower centre and the seven red diamonds.

6 Use deckle-edged scissors to cut a strip of orange foam to fit across the top of the pot.

7 Glue the flower, stem and pot face down on to the card, so that the ballpoint pen lines do not show. Glue the flower centre on to the flower, and the decoration on to the pot.

Making the square card

1 Use a craft knife and cutting mat to cut a rectangle 30x15cm (12x6in) from purple corrugated card. Score and fold the card in half in the same way as for the rectangular card.

2 Cut a 12x12cm (4³/₄x4³/₄in) square of red paper using deckle-edged scissors. Glue it on to the front of the card using spray adhesive.

3 Make individual tracings of the small flower pot pieces on the opposite page.

4 Lay the flower on to blue foam, and draw round the edge using a ballpoint pen. Cut out the flower using a craft knife and cutting mat. Now draw round and cut out the other shapes in the same way: green foam for the stem and leaves; pink for the flower centre and the six diamonds on the pot; orange for the leaf markings; and yellow for the pot.

5 Use the deckle-edged scissors to cut a purple foam strip to fit across the pot.

6 Glue the flower, stem, leaves and pot face down on to the the card, so that the pen lines do not show. Glue the flower centre on to the flower, and the decoration on to the pot.

Making the gift tags

1 Make a tracing of the gift tag opposite. Cut one tag from red corrugated card, and one from yellow. Use a hole punch to make a hole in the pointed end of each tag.

2 Make a tracing of the two single flowers, and the flower centres, on the opposite page.

3 Cut one flower from yellow foam, and the other from pink. The round centres should be cut from blue and orange foam. Glue the flowers and flower centres on to the tags.

4 Cut two lengths of ribbon 24cm (9¹/₂in) long, one in green and one in blue. Thread the ribbon through the holes in the tags.

Large Flower Pot

Small Flower Pot

Flower for Tag

Diamond for Pot
Decoration

Tag

Use these shapes to decorate
your cards. Make tracings of the
individual parts and then cut from
coloured foam. Cut the tag from
corrugated card.

Miniature Scrap Cards

You can make miniature cards using almost any small objects or scraps of fabric. Experiment with materials in new and interesting ways, combining different textures and colours. Raid the cupboard for a single button, an odd earring or a scrap of favourite fabric; the only limit is your imagination!

You will need

- Craft paper – a selection of colours
- Card – a selection of colours
- Paper – handmade, wrapping, fluorescent
- Corrugated card
- Sheet of gold paper with punched out stars
- Cork sheeting – thin
- Small objects – dried flowers, odd earrings, wooden shapes, beads, buttons, mosaic tiles, shells, stones
- Fabric – small patterned
- Coloured ribbon, coloured string
- Needle and thread – gold
- Metallic pen – gold
- Deckle-edged scissors, ballpoint pen, white paper
- Pencil, ruler, craft knife, cutting mat
- Thin wadding

Making cards

1 Draw a 18x18cm (7x7in) square on to coloured craft paper. Cut out the square using a craft knife, ruler and cutting mat.

2 Fold the paper in half, lining up the edges exactly before pressing along the folded edge. Fold the card in half again, lining up the edges before pressing along the folded edge.

Making window cards

1 Make a tracing of the rectangular or arch shaped window frame on page 27 on to white paper, and then cut out the frame and the opening making a complete window shaped template. Lay the template on to coloured card and draw around the outer and inner edges.

2 Choose a piece of patterned fabric to fit behind the window opening. Glue the fabric on to the back of the window frame. Cut a piece of thin wadding to the same size as the window opening. Place the wadding behind the opening, then glue the frame to the card so that the wadding and the fabric edges are sandwiched between the frame and the card.

Tearing handmade paper

1 When using handmade paper on these miniature cards, the edges of the paper should be torn and not cut to give a natural

look. Fold the handmade paper where you want the tear to be and then dampen with water. Tear the paper slowly along the fold which will give a very rough edge. For a slightly neater finish, hold a straight edge lightly on the fold, then tear, using the ruler as a guide (see Handmade Paper Card, page 9).

Using a metallic pen

1 Before drawing lines on to the front of your card, you must first check that the ink from your pen will not spread when applied to the surface of the paper. Practise drawing lines on a scrap of the same paper you will be using for the card. The lines can be straight, dashed, dotted or drawn freehand. If you are using a ruler, make sure that it is turned on to its concave side, or the ink may smudge when the pen is pressed against the edge of the ruler.

Decorating the cards

1 Tear a rectangle of brown wrapping paper 6x6cm (2³⁄₈x2³⁄₈in) and glue it diagonally on to the front of a blue card. Tear a rectangle of green handmade paper 4x4cm (1¹⁄₂x1¹⁄₂in) and glue it to the centre of the brown paper. Glue

an odd earring, jewel or flat metal object to the centre of the card.

2 Use deckle-edged scissors to cut four 7.5cm (3in) strips from the edge of a piece of thin cork sheeting: this make strips with one straight edge and one patterned. Glue the strips around the edge of a brown card to make a frame. Cut small triangles from a sheet of punched gold stars to fit each corner, then glue them in place. Use the deckle-edged scissors to cut a 3x3cm (1¹⁄₄x1¹⁄₄in) square from the cork sheeting. Glue this diagonally on to the centre of the card. Cut a square of punched gold stars slightly smaller than the cork, then glue it in place. Glue a cream fish shaped button on to the centre of the card.

3 Make a black window frame, with four small panes. Draw gold pen lines around each pane, and around the outer edge of the frame. Glue fabric with a small pattern on to the reverse side of the frame. Glue the frame on to the middle of a red card.

4 Make a church window frame from mauve paper using the outline on the opposite page. Select a piece of black and gold star fabric, and place it behind the opening in the frame. Cut a piece of wadding the same size as the hole cut in the frame, and place it on the back of the fabric. Glue the frame in the bottom left corner of the card. Thread a large eyed needle with gold embroidery thread, then tie a knot in the end of the thread. Make long, straight stitches from the points and centre of a star, radiating outwards on to the card. Finish the stitching at the back with a knot and a dab of glue.

5 Glue a 6x6cm (2³⁄₈x2³⁄₈in) square of shocking pink card on to a blue card. Glue a small wooden heart, painted with a wash of acrylic paint, on to the centre of the card. Glue twigs or stiff raffia in a square around the heart.

6 Glue a 6x6cm (2³⁄₈x2³⁄₈in) square of torn cream handmade paper on to a light sea green card. Cut a length of green gardening string to fit just inside the edges of the cream paper. Tie the ends in a bow and glue the string to the front of the card. Glue a colour washed wooden shape to the centre of the card.

7 Choose wrapping paper with small individual images, and areas that can be used as a border. Cut four strips of the paper for the card edges with mitred 45 degree corners. Glue the border pieces around the edge of a brown card. Cut out a small image from the wrapping paper, and glue it on to the centre of the card.

8 Tear a 2.5x2.5cm (1x1in) square, and a 2.5x5.5cm (1x2¹⁄₄in) rectangle of blue handmade paper. Glue them to the front of a sea green card, in the top right and bottom left corners. Draw a dashed gold metallic line around the blue paper square and rectangle. Glue lengths of dried grass and seed heads on to the blue panels.

9 Cut a piece of coloured corrugated card 7.5x7.5cm (3x3in) and glue to the centre of a yellow card. Glue three mosaic tiles in the centre of the corrugated card. Glue a button or flat object on to the centre of each tile.

10 Cut a square of ginger silk fabric 4x4cm (1¹⁄₂x1¹⁄₂in) and pull away some of the thread to fray the edges. Glue the fabric on to the centre of a black card. Draw a gold line using a ruler and metallic pen around the edges of the card front. Glue a small stone or bead in the centre of the silk.

Use these outlines to make window shaped templates for your cards.

Jewelled Elephant Cards

Metal, silk and jewels have been used on these cards, to bring you a touch of the mystic east. The copper and brass elephants have a punched pattern, and are decorated with jewels and mirrors. Pieces of silk, organza, and sheer ribbon add colour and texture to these rich, sumptuous gift cards, envelopes and tags

You will need

- Card – gold, cream, pink
- Metal sheet – copper, brass
- Small circular mirrors
- Flat backed glass faceted jewels – blue, green
- Outliner paste – copper, gold
- Scraps of silk, sheer fabric and ribbon
- Richly coloured cord
- Sheer ribbon – purple
- Rubber mallet, small and medium punching tool
- Soft wooden board, hole punch, white paper
- Pencil, ruler, craft knife, cutting mat
- Scissors – large and small
- Tacky glue, hot glue gun

Making the Taj Mahal card

1 Make a tracing of the Taj Mahal card on page 33 on to white paper. If you would like the card to be the same size as it appears in this project, you will need to use a photocopier to enlarge all the tracings by 10%.

2 Lay the tracing on to cream card and cut out one complete card on the outer line of the trace. Score along the dotted line using a ruler and the back of a craft knife. Fold the card on the scored line.

3 Make a tracing of the front border edge, and then cut two from gold card. Cut one gold, back border edge in the same way.

4 Choose some richly coloured scraps of silk and sheer fabric for the backdrop of the card. Glue the fabric at the sides and in the middle of the card front, leaving a 6mm (¼in) gap around the outer edges.

5 Glue one Taj Mahal shaped gold border edge on to the front of the card to cover the fabric ends. Glue the other border edge to the inside front of the card, and the back border edge on to the inside back of the card.

6 Make tracings of the Taj Mahal central panel, arch, small elephant, and small and large teardrops on page 32 and 33. Enlarge the

tracings by the same percentage as the card. Cut out the traced shapes. Lay the tracing for the front panel, and the small elephant on to brass sheeting; and the arch, and small and large teardrops on to copper sheeting. Draw around the tracings using a ballpoint pen, transferring the outlines to the metal sheet. Use scissors to cut out one of each shape, and two small teardrops.

7 Place the brass elephant on to a soft wooden board. Use a sharp punching tool and soft rubber mallet to make small holes around the outer edge of the elephant (see Cutting and Punching Tin, page 10). Punch a loop of small holes for the elephant's ear. Now punch holes around the edges of the other shapes in the same way, using both the small and medium punching tool.

8 Use the glue gun to attach the copper arch, and the large and two small teardrops to the brass central panel. Glue the panel to the front of the card. Glue an arch shaped piece of richly coloured fabric, then the brass elephant on to the copper arch.

9 Cut scraps of fabric for the elephant's saddle and head decoration. Glue them on to the elephant. Glue five small circular mirrors overlapping the borders of the card. Glue green and blue flat-backed faceted jewels either side of the mirrors, and on the tear-drop shaped copper panel.

10 Use copper outliner paste to add detail lines to the elephant, his saddle and ear, and to dot his eye. Outline the mirrors, the inner edge of the border, and the outer edge of the card. Squeeze the outliner paste tube gently, keeping your hand steady, as if using an icing tube.

Making the envelope

1 Using the design for the envelope on page 63 as a guide, draw a rectangle on gold card, slightly larger than your card. Add flaps to the rectangle to make an envelope shape. Cut out the envelope, then score and fold on the dotted lines. Fold the side flaps in, and the bottom up, and glue together.

2 Cut a 5x5.5cm (2x2$\frac{1}{4}$in) rectangle from copper sheet. Make and decorate a small brass elephant. Glue the copper rectangle, the fabric, and the elephant on to the envelope.

3 Make a seal for the back of the envelope using a small square of punched copper sheeting. Cut a piece of fabric slightly smaller than the copper square, and a tear-drop shape from brass sheet. Punch the edges of the metal, then glue the fabric and the tear-drop on to the copper rectangle. Decorate with a small circular mirror outlined with copper coloured outliner paste, then glue to the back of the envelope.

Making the gift tag

1 Cut a 7x7cm (2$\frac{3}{4}$x2$\frac{3}{4}$in) square of gold card. Punch two holes on one edge.

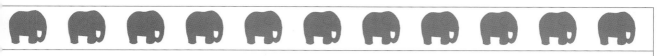

2 Cut out a copper rectangle 5x5.5cm (2x2¼in), and decorate the edges with punched holes. Make a small brass elephant in the same way as for the envelope. Glue the copper rectangle, a slightly smaller piece of fabric and the elephant on to the tag. Thread a length of cord through the holes and seal the ends together using a hot glue gun.

Making the elephant stack

1 Make a tracing of the elephant stack card on page 32 on to white paper. Enlarge it by 10% on a photocopier. Lay the tracing on to cream card and cut out one complete card. Score along the dotted line using a ruler and the back of a craft knife. Fold the card on the scored line. Make tracings of the front, and the back border edges, and then cut from gold card.

2 Choose some richly coloured scraps of silk and sheer fabric for the backdrop of the card. Glue the fabric pieces to the front of the cream coloured card in the same way as for the Taj Mahal card.

3 Glue one of the two shaped gold border edges to the front of the card to cover the fabric ends. Glue the second on to the inside front of the card, and the square border edge on to the inside back.

4 Make tracings of the stacked elephant design on page 33. Enlarge to the same size as before. Cut out the traced shapes. Place the tracing on to brass sheeting and then draw round the edge of the elephants using a ballpoint pen. Use scissors to cut out the stacked elephant shape.

5 Place the brass elephant stack on to a soft wooden board and punch holes. Decorate the elephant stack using scraps of fabric, then glue to the centre of the card.

6 Decorate the card frame with green and blue glass flat-backed jewels. Decorate the jewels, frame and the elephants using gold outliner paste.

Making the envelope

1 Using the envelope design on page 63 as a guide, cut out the envelope from pink coloured card. Fold then glue the envelope together. Make a tracing of the two smaller elephants from the elephant stack, then cut out the elephants from brass sheeting. Decorate with fabric and outliner paste in the same way as before, then glue them to the front of the envelope.

Making the gift tag

1 Cut a rectangle of gold card, and punch two holes on one short edge. Cut a square of fabric, to fit diagonally on to the tag. Make and decorate a small elephant. Glue the fabric and the elephant on to the tag. Thread a length of purple ribbon through the holes in the tag, then join the ends with a knot. Glue a large glass jewel on to the ribbon, between the holes. Decorate the tag with gold outliner paste.

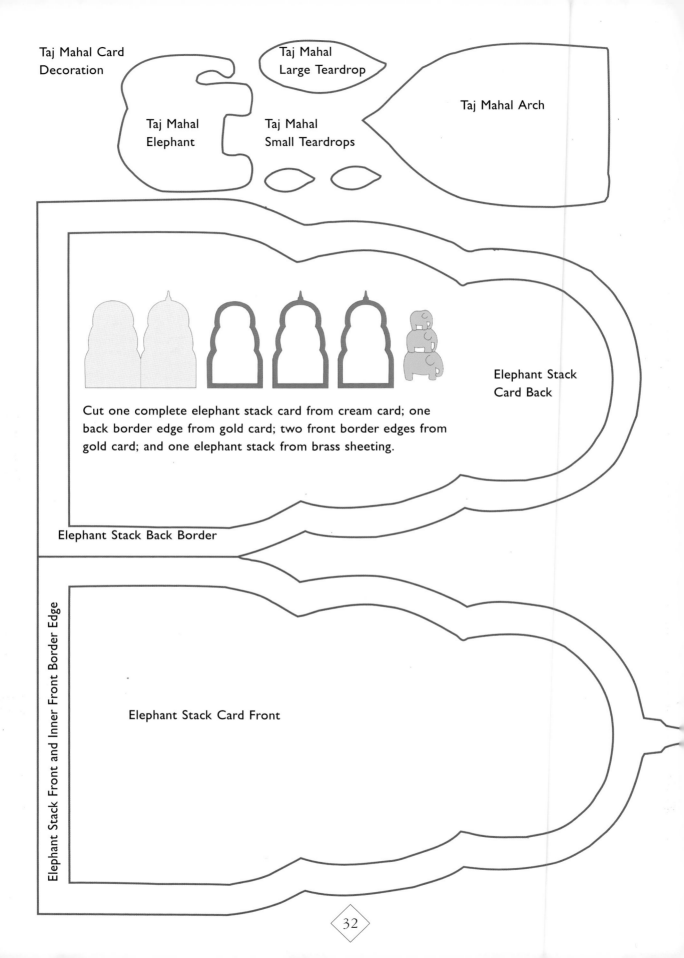

Taj Mahal Card
Decoration

Taj Mahal
Large Teardrop

Taj Mahal Arch

Taj Mahal
Elephant

Taj Mahal
Small Teardrops

Cut one complete elephant stack card from cream card; one
back border edge from gold card; two front border edges from
gold card; and one elephant stack from brass sheeting.

Elephant Stack
Card Back

Elephant Stack Back Border

Elephant Stack Front and Inner Front Border Edge

Elephant Stack Card Front

Cut one complete Taj Mahal card from cream card; one back border edge from gold card; two front border edges from gold card; one central panel and one elephant from brass sheeting; one arch, one large tear-drop and two small tear-drops from copper sheeting.

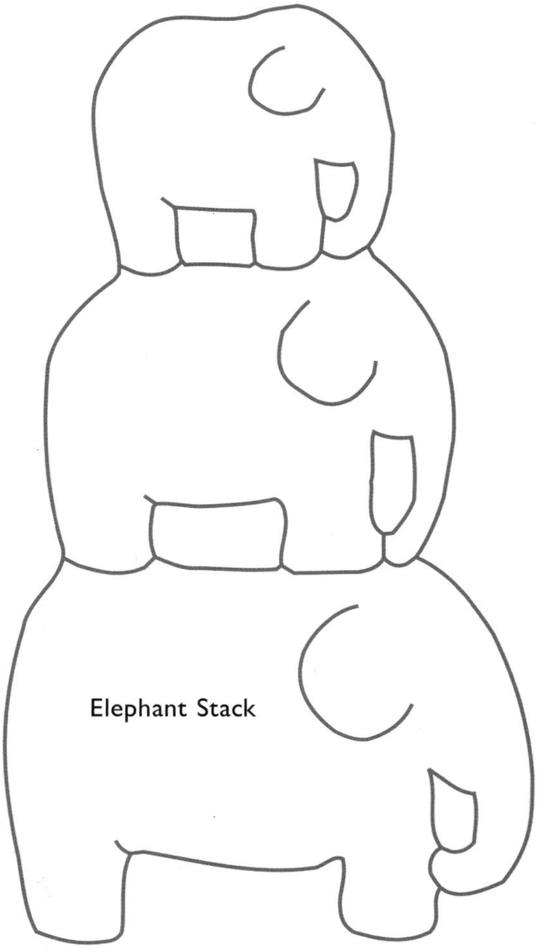

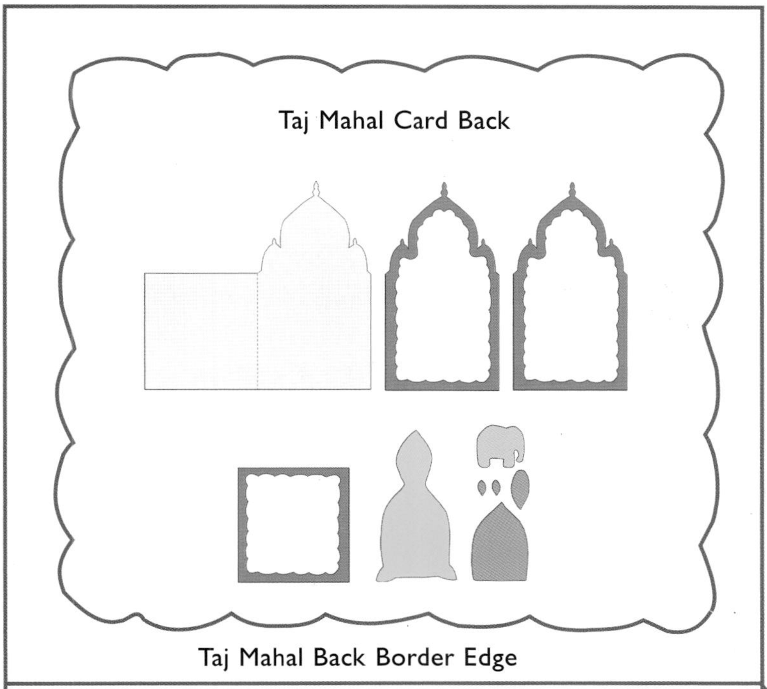

Taj Mahal Card Back

Taj Mahal Back Border Edge

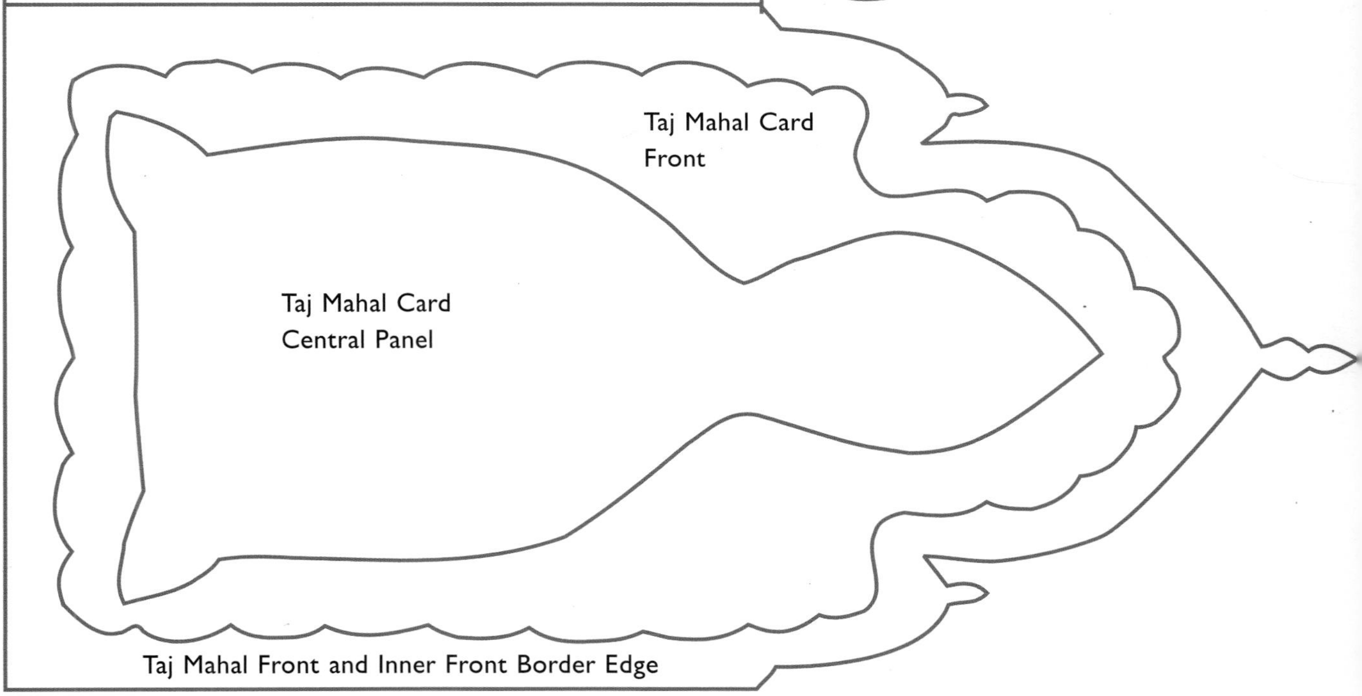

Elephant Stack

Taj Mahal Card Front

Taj Mahal Card Central Panel

Taj Mahal Front and Inner Front Border Edge

Window Cards

These beautifully painted cards with their clear windows, opening shutters and curtains are wonderful to send a greeting for any occasion. One card looks from the garden towards the inside of the house; the other is a room inside the house with pretty curtains, wall paper, and two cats sitting in the sun on the window sill

You will need

- Thick watercolour paper – white
- Acetate sheet – clear
- Thin foam sheeting – white
- Outliner paste – silver, white
- Acrylic paints – light green, dark green, pink, white, terracotta, dark brown, ginger, black, grey
- Watercolour pencils – light green, dark green, yellow, light blue, dark blue, grey, purple
- Two beads – purple
- Fabric – orange, sheer green
- Craft wire – black
- Embroidery thread – green
- Ruler, craft knife, cutting mat, pencil
- Tacky glue, hot melt glue gun
- Container of clean water
- Paintbrushes, kitchen cloths

Making the shutters card

1 Use a craft knife and cutting mat to cut a rectangle 22x32cm (8³⁄₄x12³⁄₄in) from thick white watercolour paper. Score and fold the card in half (see Making a Card Mount, page 12). Turn the card to the landscape position. Draw a rectangle in faint pencil, 3.5cm (1³⁄₄in) in from the edges of the card. Cut out the rectangle using a craft knife and cutting mat.

2 Cut another rectangle of water-colour paper just larger than the rectangle you have cut from the front of the card. Draw a rectangle 1cm (³⁄₈in) in from the edges of this piece of paper, and cut it out: this is the window frame. Glue the frame inside the card behind the window opening cut in the card.

3 Glue a piece of clear acetate inside the card behind the window opening. Use silver outliner paste to draw grid lines of panes on to the window. Leave to dry.

4 Cut two rectangles of watercolour paper 10x12cm (4x4³⁄₄in) for the shutters. Use the back of a craft knife and a straight edge to score a line, 1cm (³⁄₈in) from one long edge on each rectangle. This will create a tab that can be glued to the card, and will allow the shutters to open and close. Use a dark blue watercolour pencil to draw a rectangle 1cm (³⁄₈in) in from the edges on both sides of each

shutter. Draw a line around the edge of each shutter, then draw evenly spaced lines horizontally in the rectangle in the centre of each side of the shutter. Use a light blue water-colour pencil to shade between each slat, and around the border. Once you are happy with the effect, dip a paintbrush into water and wet the shutters a section at a time to transform the pencil shading into watercolour paint. Leave until dry and then glue both shutters by their tabs, either side of the window opening. Glue a small wooden bead on to the outside of each shutter for a handle.

5 Use watercolour pencils to draw in a window ledge and bricks on to the wall. Paint with water and leave to dry.

Making the curtains

1 Cut a rectangle of fabric the same width as the window, but a little longer in length, then cut the material in half. Place the fabric face down on to the inside of the card. Use a hot melt glue gun to attach the outside edges of the fabric to the card. Gather the fabric at either side of the window, securing it at the

top with glue, and add a few blobs at the bottom to hold the folds in place. Cut a pelmet from the same fabric, gather it up and then glue it along the top of the window.

Making the plants and cat

1 Make tracings of the pots and large cat on the opposite page on to white paper. Cut out the designs, and lay them on to a piece of thin white foam. Draw round the shapes using a ballpoint pen, then cut out using a craft knife and cutting mat.

2 Paint the pots using terracotta coloured acrylic paint, adding shading using white and dark brown. Paint spots of green for the foliage and spots of bright pink for the geranium flowers. Fill the white spaces between the flowers and leaves with dark green paint. When the paint is dry, add dots of white to the flower heads. Paint the other pot of pansies using purple, yellow and greens.

3 Paint the cat with black acrylic and leave to dry. Use an old stiff brush to drag warm brown, ginger and white on to the cat for his fur. Outline the edge of the cat, and his features, using a fine brush and black acrylic paint.

4 Glue the three pots of flowers and the cat on to the window ledge. Use medium green, dark green, mauve and pink acrylic to paint branches of wistaria trailing over the top of the window. Add a few geranium petals to the window sill, and a vase of flowers on the inside of the window, painted on to the acetate.

Making the indoor cat card

1 Use a craft knife and cutting mat to cut a rectangle 22x32cm (8³/₄inx12³/₄in) from thick watercolour paper. Score and fold the card in the same way as before, then turn the card to the landscape position. Cut a 12.5x8.5cm (5x3¹/₄in)

window in the centre of the card. Glue clear acetate on to the inside of the window, adding a grid of lines using white outliner paste.

2 Use watercolour pencils to draw a rectangle underneath the window for the sill, and two lines 1cm (³/₈in) apart, horizontally across the card for the wallpaper border. Above this, make random patches using a lemon yellow watercolour pencil. Dip a paintbrush in water and blend the patches to create a colour washed effect. Leave to dry, then add clusters of small green dots at regular intervals over the wash. Below the border draw vertical stripes, 1cm (³/₈in) apart in green watercolour pencil. Colour alternate stripes lemon yellow, adding shading using dark green. To the other stripes add swirls of lime green with a dark green shadow. Paint the border in the same way with green swirls. Paint a little water over the stripes and border, then leave the card to dry.

Making the curtains

1 Make a curtain pole by twisting together two 17cm (6³/₄in) lengths of black craft wire. Curl the ends into hooks.

2 Cut two pieces of sheer green fabric for the curtains. Cut small slits vertically along the top of the fabric then feed the curtain pole through the slits. Gather up the curtains either side of the curtain pole, then glue the curtains to the top and side edges of the window using a glue gun. Cut a piece of sheer fabric for the pelmet, and wrap it around the pole. Glue the back of the pelmet and the pole to the top of the window. Use a length of embroidery thread to tie back each curtain.

Making the cats and pot

1 Cut out one small plant pot and a pair of black and white cats, and paint in the same way as for the other card. Glue the pot and the cats on to the window sill.

Use these outlines to make tracings for cutting the pots and cats from white foam.

Happy Clown Cards

These fun clowns can be used to decorate birthday cards or gift bags. The clowns are built up in layers of thin foam, which is mounted on to a psychedelic paper background. Moving toy eyes and pom poms complete the cards, making the clowns look lively enough to jump right off the page, and join the party fun

You will need

- Strong white card
- White paper gift bag – 20x26cm (8x10in)
- Coloured foam sheeting – yellow, purple, red, orange, pink, light green, dark green, light blue, dark blue, white
- Medium pom poms – green, red, purple, yellow, pink, blue, orange
- Small pom poms – red, green, yellow
- Chenille sticks – blue, orange, green, red
- Psychedelic printed paper – blue, pink, green
- Toy eyes – three pairs
- Acrylic paint – red, yellow, white
- Permanent marker pen – black
- Pencil, ruler, scissors, ballpoint pen – black
- Craft knife, cutting mat, white paper
- Tacky glue

Making the umbrella clown

1 Use a craft knife and cutting mat to cut a rectangle 22x29cm (8½x11½in) from strong white card. Draw a fine pencil line midway across the width of the card. Score along this line using a straight edge and the back of a craft knife (see Making a Card Mount, page 12). Fold the card in half, pressing along the score line.

2 Cut a piece of blue psychedelic paper 22x14.5cm (8½x5¾in) and glue it to the front of the card. If your paper is smaller than this, use more than one piece and overlap, matching the edges.

3 Use a pencil and ruler to draw a rectangular window in the centre front of the card, 3.5cm (1⅜in) in from each edge. Open the card and cut out the window using a craft knife, straight edge and cutting mat.

4 Trace the outline of the umbrella clown on page 42 on to white paper; do not add any detail lines. Cut out the tracing and lay it on to a piece of white foam. Use a ballpoint pen to draw around the outside edge, transferring the shape to the foam. Cut out the umbrella clown using a craft knife and cutting mat. Glue the white foam shape on to the card, using the main picture opposite as a positional guide: this will be the base for the coloured foam shapes.

5 Each coloured part of the clown must have its own tracing, so make individual tracings on to white paper of the top and base of the umbrella, two hair pieces, mouth, jacket, shirt front, trousers, puddle and sock stripes.

6 Lay the individual tracing on to coloured foam, draw around the edges and cut the following pieces: blue for the puddle; purple for the trousers; red for the jacket, sock stripes and mouth; yellow for the shirt front; orange for the hair pieces; and the top of the umbrella in light green and the underside in dark green.

7 Glue the coloured foam pieces on the white clown base using tacky glue. The face, hands and alternate sock stripes will remain white, and will not be covered by a second layer of foam.

8 Use a permanent black marker pen to draw an outline around each piece of the clown's clothing, hair, umbrella and puddle, then add the detail lines using the picture on the opposite page as a guide.

9 Use acrylic paints to add red stripes to the clown's shirt, yellow spots to his jacket and

to paint his trouser patches yellow and red. Glue a pair of toy eyes on to the clown's face, and a small red pom pom for his nose.

10 Glue orange chenille stick around the front and bottom of the clown's coat; blue for the outer edge of the window opening; and black for the umbrella handle. Glue a medium purple pom pom on to the clown's jacket as a button, and red, orange, yellow and blue pom poms alternately around the edge of the card.

Making the happy clown

1 Cut a 16x24cm (6¼x9½in) rectangle of white card. Score and fold the card in half in the same way as the umbrella clown card.

2 Cut a piece of pink psychedelic paper 12x16cm (4¾x6¼in) and glue it to the front of the card.

3 Use a pencil and ruler to draw and then cut out a rectangular window in the centre front of the card, 2.5cm (1in) from each edge.

4 Make a tracing of the happy clown outline on page 43. Cut a complete clown shape from white foam, in the same way as for the umbrella clown. Glue the white foam clown across the hole cut in the card.

5 Make individual tracings of the different coloured clown parts. Use the tracings to cut the parts from coloured foam: blue for the hat; orange for the hair pieces; white for the ruff; red for the mouth; and pink and mauve for the stripes on the shirt.

6 Glue the coloured foam pieces on to white clown base using tacky glue. The face and hands will remain white and not be covered by a second layer of foam.

7 Use the permanent black marker pen to draw an outline around each piece of the clown's clothing, hair, hat and ruff. Use yellow acrylic paint to add spots to the clown's hat, and stripes to his shirt. Glue a pair of toy eyes to the clown's face, and a small red pom pom for his nose.

8 Glue two medium blue pom poms on to the clown's shirt as buttons, and trim his hat, cuffs and the edge of his coat with alternate green and yellow pom poms. Glue green chenille stick around the edge of the clown's ruff.

Making the balloon clown

1 Cut a piece of green psychedelic paper 15x19.5cm (6x7½in) and glue it to the centre of the front of a white paper gift bag. Cut a piece of strong white card 9x13cm (3½x5¼in) and glue it to the centre of the psychedelic paper. Trim the edge of the white card with blue chenille sticks.

2 Make a tracing of the balloon clown outline on page 43, but do not include the balloons. Cut a complete clown shape from white foam. Glue the white foam shape on to the centre of the bag.

3 Make individual tracings of the clown parts and balloons. Use the tracings to cut the different parts from coloured foam: pink for the central balloon; blue for the left balloon and the clown's trousers; mauve for the right

41

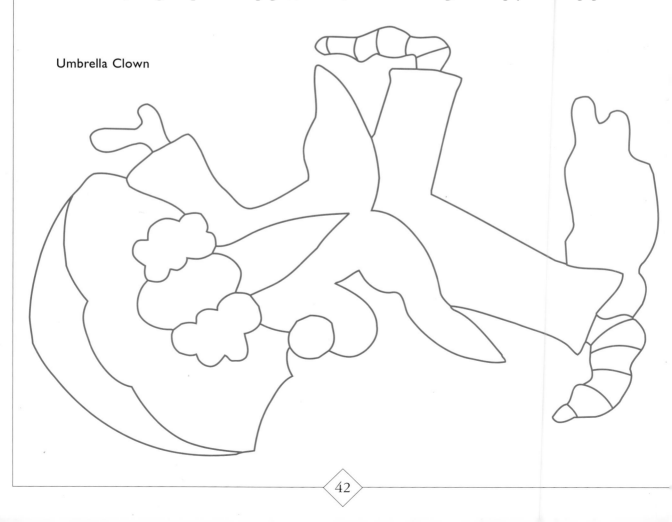

balloon, hat and clown's feet; orange for the hair; red for the flowers, mouth, bow tie; and dark blue for the triangular trouser pieces, either side of his shirt.

4 Glue the coloured foam parts on to the white clown, and the balloons just above his raised hand. The hands and face will remain white, and not be covered by a second layer of foam. Glue a piece of red chenille stick between the balloons and the clown's hand, taking the loose end past his hand. Cut a small piece of red chenille stick and glue it on to the hand holding the balloons.

5 Use the permanent black marker pen to draw an outline around all the clown pieces, and to add detail lines, using the picture on page 39 as

a guide. Use the yellow, red and white acrylic paint to colour the patch on the clown's trousers, and to add highlights to the balloons.

6 Glue a pair of toy eyes on to the clown's face, and a small red pom pom for his nose. Glue the small red flower on to one side of his hat and the larger flower on the left hand side of the clown. Glue lengths of blue chenille stick on to the clown for his belt and braces.

7 Glue a small yellow pom pom on to the flower on the clown's hat, and a medium yellow for the other flower; a medium red at the bottom of each brace, and on the middle of the bow tie; and green, red, yellow and mauve pom poms for his buttons, and alternately around the edge of the psychedelic paper.

Umbrella Clown

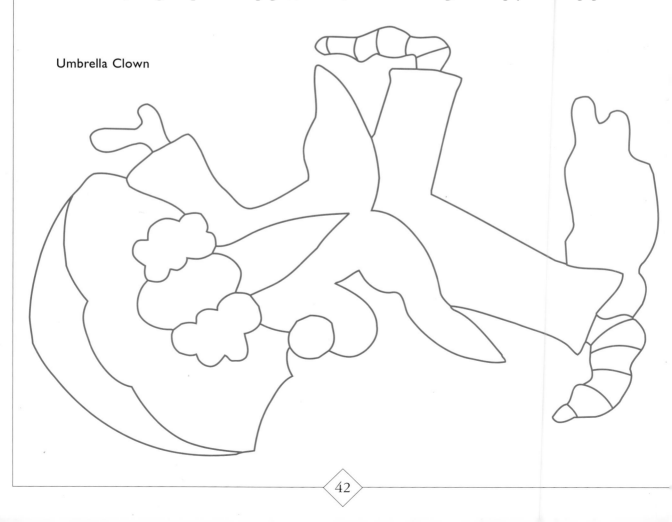

Use these outlines to cut a complete clown shape from white foam, and then to cut the individual clown parts from coloured foam.

Balloon Clown

Happy Clown

Flora and Fauna Cards

Handmade paper, dried flowers, twigs and raffia have been used to make these natural looking cards, envelopes and tags. Decorated with fruit, butterflies and ladybirds cut from handmade paper, they are sure to be a hit with anyone who enjoys nature and the countryside

You will need

- Handmade paper – dark green, light green, natural, light blue, red, mustard yellow, mauve, terracotta, cream, light brown
- Light card – brown
- Twigs, cinnamon sticks, dried flowers, bark, straw
- Natural raffia – open-weave hessian
- Hole punch
- Craft wire – thin
- Permanent marker pen – black
- Ruler, pencil, craft knife, cutting mat, scissors
- Tacky glue

Making the pineapple card

1 Use a pencil and ruler to draw a rectangle 15x25cm (6x10in) on to terracotta coloured handmade paper. Fold and dampen the paper along the pencil lines, then tear out the rectangle working against a straight edge. This will give the edges a natural torn finish (see Handmade Paper Card, page 9).

2 Tear a rectangle of natural coloured paper 8.5x10.5cm ($3^{1}/_{2}$x$4^{1}/_{8}$in). Glue it on to the centre front of the card.

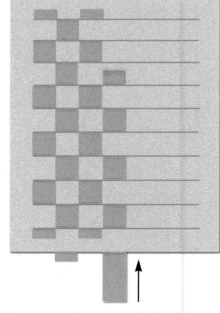

3 The pineapples are made from woven paper; either buy the paper ready made, or make

6 Cut three lengths of twig or cinnamon stick 6cm (2³/₈in) long, and glue these on to the two short sides and top of the card.

Making the envelope

1 Using the design for the envelope on page 63 as a guide, draw a rectangle slightly larger than your card, adding flaps so that when folded over will make an envelope shape. Cut out the envelope, then score and fold on the dotted lines. Fold the side flaps in, and the bottom up, and glue the envelope together.

2 Tear a piece of terracotta coloured handmade paper 5x6cm (2x2³/₈in) and glue this to the top left hand corner of the envelope. Tear a slightly smaller piece of natural coloured paper and glue this to the centre of the terracotta paper. Use the small pineapple trace on page 48 to cut the pineapple from basket weave paper, and the top from dark and light green paper. Glue the complete pineapple over the rectangle of handmade paper in the corner of the envelope.

Making the gift tag

1 Tear a piece of terracotta coloured paper 7x9cm (2³/₄x3¹/₂in) and make a hole in one corner using a hole punch. Tear a piece of natural coloured paper 5x6.5cm (2x2¹/₂in) and glue it to the centre of the terracotta paper.

2 Cut a pineapple from basket weave paper, and the pineapple top from dark and light paper, using the medium sized pineapple design on page 48. Glue the pineapple in position on the tag, then thread the tag with a length of raffia.

Making the apple card

1 Tear a rectangle 15x25cm (6x10in) of green handmade paper. Score and fold the card in the same way as for the pineapple card. Tear a

your own. To do this cut two pieces of thin handmade paper 15x20cm (6x8in), one in cream and one in light brown. Take the light brown piece and draw a rectangle 1cm (³/₈in) in from the edges using a pencil and ruler. Mark off 6mm (¹/₄in) intervals down both short sides of the rectangle. Cut parallel slits within the rectangle, joining the marks together on both sides. Now cut strips of cream paper, 6mm (¹/₄in) wide and 15cm (6in) long. Weave the lighter strips up between the strips cut in light brown paper forming a basket weave effect.

4 Make tracings of the pineapples on page 48. Cut out the shapes, then lay them on to the basket weave paper. Draw around the outside edge of the pineapples, and then cut around the edge. Once you have cut out the basket weave pineapples, you may need to add a small amount of glue to the edges of the paper strips to hold the pineapples together.

5 Make tracings of the pineapple tops. Cut the larger tops from dark green paper and the smaller insides from light green. Cut two narrow strips of dark green paper to go down the centre of the tops. Glue the pieces on to the front of the card.

rectangle of natural coloured paper 8x12cm (3¼x4¾in), and glue it to the centre front of the card.

2 Cut a piece of thin flat bark or ridged brown paper 8x10cm (3¼x4in) and glue it over the natural coloured paper. Make a bow from several lengths of raffia and glue it to the top left hand corner of the bark.

3 Cut the apples and leaves from light green handmade paper. Cut the leaf veins from dark green and the highlights on the apples in white. Glue the apples and leaves on to the front of the card. Cut short lengths of twig or cinnamon stick for the stems, and glue them to the tops and bottoms of the apples.

Making the envelope and tag

1 Make an envelope in the same way as for the pineapple card, adding a rectangle of green and natural paper, and a small apple.

2 Tear a rectangle of natural coloured paper 6.5x8cm (2½x3¼in). Make the tag in the same way as for the pineapple, adding a rectangle of green paper, and a small apple.

Making the ladybird card

1 Tear a rectangle 15x25cm (6x10in) from grey coloured paper. Score and fold the card in the same way as for the pineapple card. Tear a rectangle of green paper 8x10cm (3¼x4in) and glue it to the centre front of the card.

2 Cut a clover leaf shape from light green paper. Glue this to the card, adding leaf veins in dark green paper. Use the designs on page 49 to cut a large and a medium ladybird from red paper. Glue the ladybirds on to the card, then add spots, head and tail markings, and feet using a black permanent marker pen.

3 Glue two small pieces of twig or cinnamon stick in opposite corners of the card.

Making the envelope and tag

1 Make an envelope in the same way as for the pineapple card, adding a rectangle of green handmade paper, a small green clover leaf, and a small ladybird.

2 Tear a rectangle of dark green paper 7x8cm (2¾x3¼in). Make the tag in the same way as for the pineapple tag, adding a small clover leaf and medium and a very small ladybirds.

Making the butterfly card

1 Tear a rectangle 15x25cm (6x10in) from mustard yellow handmade paper. Cut a square of open weave hessian 9x11cm (3½x4½in) and glue to the centre of the card.

2 Use the design on page 49 to cut a leaf from green paper. Glue a length of thin craft wire on to the back of the leaf for the spine. Make vein marks on the leaf using a blunt tool. Glue the leaf, and a spray of dried flowers, on to the hessian.

3 Cut a butterfly from mauve coloured paper, the markings from dark blue, and a body from cream. Use a dark blue pencil to add detail lines to the butterfly wings. Glue the butterfly on to the card adding two lengths of straw for antennae.

Making the envelope and tag

1 Make an envelope in the same way as for the pineapple card, adding a rectangle of yellow handmade paper, and a small butterfly.

2 Tear a rectangle of yellow paper 7x8cm (2¾x3¼in). Make the tag in the same way as for the pineapple, adding a small rectangle of hessian and a small butterfly.

Small Apple

Apples

Medium
Pineapple

Use these outlines
to make tracings
for your flora and
fauna cards.

Pineapples

Small
Pineapple

48

Small Clover Leaf

Medium Clover Leaf

Clover Leaf

Small
Butterfly

Leaf

Butterfly

Ladybird

Very
Small

Small
Ladybird

Medium
Ladybird

Plant Display Cards

These pretty display cards with pots of flowers are just the thing to give a keen gardener for a birthday gift. Fill the pots with a selection of small dried flowers; then once the birthday is over, the card can be framed and hung in the conservatory or garden room as a year-round reminder of summer in the garden

You will need

- Card – cream, light green, dark green, light blue, turquoise and terracotta
- Dried flowers
- Self-adhesive sticky pads
- Double-sided sticky tape
- Pencil, ballpoint pen, white paper
- Ruler, white paper
- Scissors
- Craft knife, cutting mat, ruler
- Tacky glue

Making the card

1 Cut a rectangle of pale coloured card 16.5x17cm (6$\frac{1}{2}$x6$\frac{3}{4}$in). Draw a fine pencil line midway across the width of the card. Score along this line using a straight edge and the back of a craft knife (see Making a Card Mount, page 12). Fold the card along the score line. Make the larger card in the same way using a 24x17cm (9$\frac{1}{2}$x6$\frac{3}{4}$in) rectangle of card.

2 Make a tracing of the large or small card design on pages 52 and 53 on to white paper using a ballpoint pen. Place the tracing on to the front of the folded card and draw over the dotted lines, pressing hard enough to make indentations in the card. Draw over the indentations with a pencil. Cut out the marked rectangle in the centre of the card: this will be the window opening. Use the tracing to cut a window frame from coloured card. Glue the frame over the opening on the front of the card.

3 Make a tracing of the large or small canopy on page 53. Transfer the design lines on to card, and cut out the canopy. Score along the dotted line at the top, and then fold the tab over on to the reverse side. Make a crease along the lower dotted line. Glue the tab to the card using double-sided sticky tape: the top of the canopy should be level with the card top. Attach the bottom edge of the canopy to the card using self-adhesive sticky pads.

4 Make a tracing of the large or small steps on the opposite page. Transfer the design lines to coloured card, and cut out the steps. Score along the dotted lines, then fold the top and bottom tabs over on to the back of the steps, before concertina folding along the remaining score lines to make steps.

5 Attach a row of self-adhesive sticky pads across the card, 1.25cm (1/2in) below the pencil line drawn across the bottom of the card. Use double sided sticky tape to attach the top and bottom tabs on the back of the steps to the card, so that the top step is level with the pencil line and supported on the sticky pads.

6 Make a tracing of the plant pot and another of the plant pot rim on the opposite page. Use the tracings to cut the pot and the rim from terracotta coloured card. Glue the rim on to the pot. Make a small slit in the pot just above the rim, which is shown as a dotted line on the diagram.

7 Cut dried flowers into short lengths and insert the stems through the slit at the top of the pot. Glue the stems on to the back of the pot. Make three pots for the smaller card, and five for the larger. Attach them on to the steps using self-adhesive sticky pads which will space them away from the card.

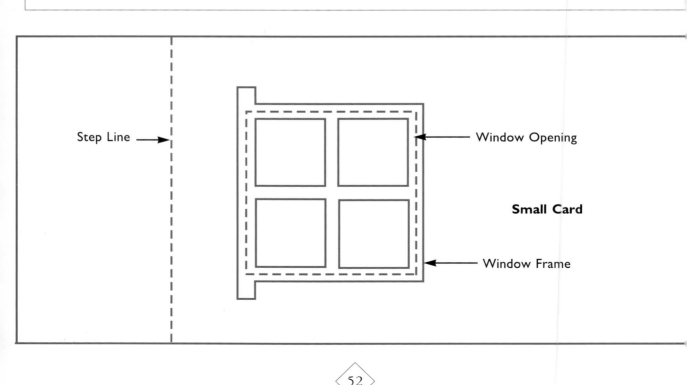

Step Line →

Window Opening

Small Card

Window Frame

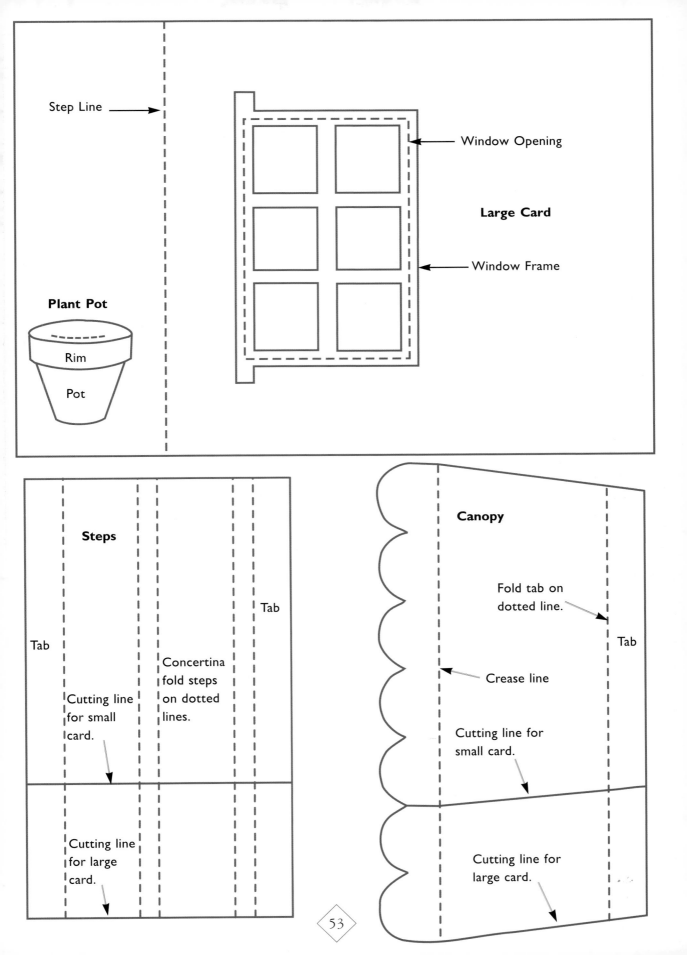

Step Line

Window Opening

Large Card

Window Frame

Plant Pot

Rim

Pot

Steps

Tab

Tab

Cutting line for small card.

Concertina fold steps on dotted lines.

Cutting line for large card.

Canopy

Fold tab on dotted line.

Tab

Crease line

Cutting line for small card.

Cutting line for large card.

53

Romantic Occasion Cards

These pretty celebration cards decorated with organza and lace make perfect gifts for weddings, anniversaries and engagements. Shades of burgundy, cream and gold give the cards a classic feel that will appeal to couples of any age; a special gift of love to give and receive

You will need

- Card – white, cream
- Scraps of organza – iridescent cream, gold
- Scraps of edging lace – white
- Organza ribbon – pink, gold
- Large-eyed needle, iridescent tissue
- Scraps of card – pale pink, deep pink
- Silk flowers and leaves – white, red
- Cardboard, pen top, cotton wool
- Fine florist's wire, craft spray paint – gold
- Acrylic paint – pink
- Spray paint – gold
- Paintbrush, soft pencil, white paper
- Straight edge, craft knife, cutting mat
- Spray adhesive, tacky glue
- Container of clean water

Making the bouquet card

1 Using a craft knife and cutting mat, cut a rectangle of cream card 22x11cm (8³/₄x4³/₈in). Draw a fine pencil line midway across the width of the card.

2 Score across this line using a straight edge and the back of the craft knife (see Making a Card Mount, page 12). The scored line should have just broken the top layer of the card, making it easier to fold in half. Practise on a scrap of card before you begin.

3 Fold the card in half, lining up the edges of the card without putting pressure on the scored line. Check the alignment at the edges then press the card along the score.

Making the bouquet

1 Roughly cut a 9cm (3¹/₂in) square of gold organza. Glue this centrally on to the front of the card with spray adhesive. Glue a length of lace, vertically, down the centre of the card front on top of the organza.

2 Bunch together a spray of small, white silk flowers and leaves. Bind the stems together by wrapping them with fine florist's wire.

3 Cut a 14cm (5¹/₂in) square of iridescent tissue. Place the bouquet on the tissue, so that the flowers lie diagonally across the centre.

4 Wrap the sides of the tissue around the flowers, and bind tightly around the stems with fine wire.

5 Cut off the tissue 2.5cm (1in) below the wire, then make a bow around the bouquet using pink ribbon.

6 Glue the bouquet diagonally on to the front of the card.

Making the gift box card

1 Cut a rectangle of white card 28x14cm (11x5½in). Score and then fold the card in half in the same way as for the bouquet card. Roughly cut a 11cm (5½in) square of cream organza. Glue it centrally to the front of the card using spray adhesive.

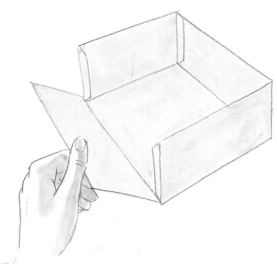

2 Make two identical boxes from thick paper or thin card. Transfer the design lines from the diagram on the opposite page on to the card or paper, using a pencil and ruler, and then cut out the shape, before folding and gluing the sides in place. When the glue is dry, spray paint the box gold. Glue a length of lace across the middle of one of the boxes: this will be the lid. Tie a small bow using pink organza ribbon, and then thread another length of

ribbon through the knot at the back using a large-eyed needle. Glue the ribbon around the box, so that it is in the centre of the lace with the bow in the middle of the box.

3 Cut four 7cm (2¾in) squares of iridescent tissue. Push them one at a time into the other box, so that they are at different angles to one another: this is the base. Add a small amount of tacky glue between the layers to hold them in place. Glue a spray of small, red silk flowers inside the base.

4 Arrange the base and lid on to the front of the card and glue in place with tacky glue: the base should be flat on the card, and one corner of the lid should be resting on the base.

Making the heart card

1 Cut a rectangle of cream card 18x16cm (7x6¼in). Score and fold the card in half in the same way as for the gift box and bouquet cards. Roughly cut a rectangle of gold coloured organza 13x6cm (5¾x2⅜in). Glue it centrally on to the front of the card using spray adhesive.

2 Using spray adhesive, glue a length of lace horizontally across the card front, slightly below the middle of the card.

3 Paint a pen top using bright pink acrylic paint, leave it to dry. You may need several coats to cover the original colour. Wrap gold coloured organza ribbon two or three times around the pen top, gluing the ribbon ends to hold them in place. Fill the pen top with cotton wool.

4 Make tracings of the large and small heart shapes on the opposite page. Transfer the outlines to pale and deep pink coloured card, and cut out the hearts. Glue a length of gold

wire on to the back of each heart. Dab glue on to each of the heart flower stems, and push them down into the cotton wool inside the painted pen top. Glue the back of the pen top to the front of the card.

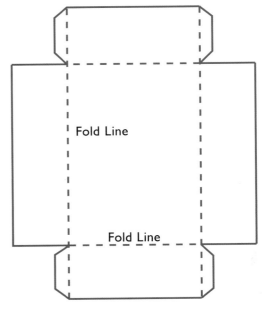

Fold Line

Fold Line

Use the heart shapes (above) and the box outline (right) to create decorations for these romantic cards

Moon and Star Cards

These celestial cards in gold and silver are quick and easy to make, yet the final results are stunning. All the cards are simply finished, but the variety of textures, including corrugated card, punched tin and holographic paper, give the cards added interest and make them easy to produce in large numbers

You will need

- Triple fold window cards – 9x12cm (3½x4½in), 8x11cm (4½x3in), 11x15.5cm (4¼x6in)
- Card – silver, dark blue, white
- Paper – dark blue
- Thick card
- Scrap card
- Stationery stars
- Holographic paper – blue
- Holographic card – white
- Curling ribbon – gold, thread – silver
- Marker pen – silver, glitter pen – silver
- Corrugated card, cellophane – blue
- Fuse wire, tin cut from a single portion cat food container
- Watercolour paper, watercolour paint,
- Container of clean water, paintbrushes
- Sun and moon shaped hole punch
- Craft knife, cutting mat, scissors
- Glue gun, tacky glue, pencil, ruler

Making the gold star card

1 Cut a piece of blue holographic paper to fit behind the opening in a 9x12cm (3½x4½in) window card. Glue it to the back of the window, inside the card. Turn one flap of the card over on to the back of the holographic paper, and glue it in place.

2 Cut three lengths of gold curling ribbon approximately 12cm (4¾in), 8cm (3in) and 6cm (2¼in) long. Attach the lengths of ribbon to the card, in the top right hand corner of the holographic paper using a gold stationery star.

3 Twist the longest length of ribbon into a spiral and secure the end to the bottom left hand corner of the card using a gold star. Twist the shortest ribbon and attach it to the bottom right hand corner with another star. Twist the last length of gold ribbon and attach it in the same way, half way up the left hand edge.

Making the shooting star card

1 Cut a rectangle 11x15cm (4¼x6in) of silver card, score and fold in half (see Making a Card, page 12).

2 Roughly tear a piece of watercolour paper to fit on to the front of the card. Use dark blue and purple watercolour paint to add a wash of colour to the paper. Leave it to dry. Make a tracing of the star numbered five on

the opposite page. Use a craft knife and cutting mat to cut out the star shape from the paper, making a star shaped stencil.

3 Lay the star stencil on to the bottom left corner of the painted watercolour paper. Use a silver metallic pen to transfer the star shape to the paper by drawing within the cut away area of the stencil. Draw three straight trail lines behind the star using the metallic pen and a ruler. Glue the watercolour paper to the front of the card.

Making the corrugated card

1 Cut a rectangle 11x15cm (4¼x6in) of blue card, score and fold in half as before. Draw a border around the edges of the card front using a silver marker pen.

2 Cut a piece of corrugated card 3x3.5cm (1¼x1½in) and colour it using the silver marker pen. Make a tracing of the star numbered five on the opposite page. Use the tracing to cut a star from corrugated card. Colour the star using silver marker pen. Cut a square of blue cellophane 2x2cm (³⁄₄x³⁄₄in). Turn the card to a landscape position and glue the silver rectangle in the top left hand corner of the card. Glue the blue cellophane square towards the top left hand corner of the corrugated card, with a silver star in the centre.

Making the five star card

1 Cut a blue rectangle of card 11x15cm (4¼x6in), score and fold in half as before.

2 Draw a rectangle on to the front of the card using a silver glitter pen and a ruler (see Drawing an Outline, page 12).

3 Make a tracing of the star numbered five on to white paper, transfer the star to white card and cut out using a craft knife and cutting

mat. Colour the star using a silver glitter pen. Cut a square of thick card small enough to fit behind the glitter star. Glue the star shaped card on to the back of the star, and then glue the star in the top left corner of the card.

4 Make stencils of the stars numbered one to four. Use these stencils to draw four stars in silver marker pen, in a straight line, radiating down from the glitter star glued in the top left corner of the card.

Making the hanging star card

1 Cut a piece of dark blue paper to fit behind the opening in a 11x15.5cm (4¼x6in) window card. Outline the card opening with a line of silver glitter.

2 Make a tracing of the star numbered six opposite. Use this tracing to cut out two star shapes from silver holographic paper. Apply silver glitter pen around the edges of both stars.

3 Cut two lengths of silver thread 5cm (2in) and 8cm (3¼in) long. Glue a piece of thread to the back of each star. Now glue the ends of the thread inside the card, so that the star hangs down in the window. Glue a piece of dark blue paper over the opening in the card, then fold in the flap and glue the card together.

Add small spots of glitter glue to the blue paper in the card window.

Making the tin star card

1 Cut a rectangle of silver card 11x15cm (4¼x6in), score and fold in half as before.

2 Tear a rectangle of dark blue paper to fit on to the card, and glue it at an angle to the

front of the card.

3 Use the tracing of the star numbered six to cut out a star from thin tin sheeting. The tin can be bought from a craft shop, or cut it from a single portion cat food tin. Put the tin star face down on a scrap of thick card, then use a pencil to draw a pattern of dots and lines on the back of the star making indentations in the tin.

4 Cut a piece of fuse wire 10cm (4in) long. Wind the wire around a knitting needle to make a stretched coil spring. Use a hot glue gun to glue the spring to the back of the star, and then the star to the blue paper on the front of the card.

Making the tin moon card

1 Cut a rectangle of silver card 11x15cm (4¼x6in), score and fold in half as before.

2 Cut a piece of dark blue paper slightly smaller than the front of the card. Glue the paper in the bottom right corner of the card, so that there is a wider border at the top and down the left side of the blue paper.

3 Make a tracing of the star numbered five and the moon, and use these tracings to cut out shapes from tin. Place the shapes face down on a scrap of card and use a pencil to make indentations on the tin star, and to draw a face on the moon. Glue the star and moon on the front of the card using a glue gun.

4 Use a sun and moon shaped hole punch to make five suns and four moons from dark blue paper. Glue them on to the border edge on the front of the card using tacky glue.

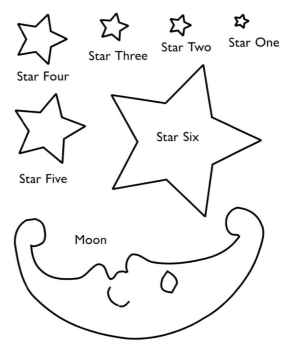

Use these outlines to cut star and moon shapes from paper, card and tin.

Acknowledgements

Thanks to the designers for contributing such wonderful projects:
Undersea World Cards (page 14), Jill Millis
Bright Daisy Cards (page 20), Cheryl Owen
Miniature Scrap Cards (page 24), Rachel Marsh
Jewelled Elephant Cards (page 28), Jill Millis
Window Cards (page 34), Jill Millis
Happy Clown Cards (page 38), Jill Millis
Flora and Fauna Cards (page 44), Jill Millis
Plant Display Cards (page 50), Cheryl Owen
Romantic Occasion Cards (page 54), Cheryl Owen
Moon and Star Cards (page 58), Jan Cox and John Underwood

Many thanks to Design Objectives for supplying Anita's acrylics
and flexible glass paint.

Other books in the Made Easy series

Decorative Papers (David & Charles, 2000)

Painted Crafts (David & Charles, 1999)

Candle Making (David & Charles, 1999)

Papier Mâché (David & Charles, 1999)

3-D Découpage (David & Charles, 1999)

Mosaics (David & Charles, 1999)

Ceramic Painting (David & Charles, 1999)

Stamping (David & Charles, 1998)

Stencilling (David & Charles, 1998)

Glass Painting (David & Charles, 1998)

Silk Painting (David & Charles, 1998)

Suppliers

ColArt Fine Art & Graphics Ltd
Whitefriars Avenue
Harrow
Middlesex HA3 5RH
Tel: 0181 4274343
Paint wholesaler, telephone for local stockist
(Acrylic paints)

Design Objectives (Head office only)
36-44 Willis Way
Fleets Industrial Estate
Poole
Dorset BH15 3SU
Tel: 01202 679976
Craft wholesaler, telephone for local stockist
(Acetate, acrylic paint, flexible glass paint,
metal sheeting, pom poms and chenille stick)

Hobby Crafts (Head office only)
River Court, Southern Sector
Bournemouth International Airport
Christchurch
Dorset BH23 6SE
Tel: 0800 272387 freephone
Retail shops nationwide, telephone for local
store
(Craft warehouse)

Fred Aldous Ltd
37 Lever Street
Manchester
M1 1LW
Tel: 0161 236 3477
Mail order service
(Craft materials)

Making an envelope
Use this outline as a guide when creating an envelope for your greeting card. Lay your card down on to thick paper. Draw a rectangle on to the paper, slightly larger than your card, then add flaps to the four edges. Score along the dotted lines; fold the side flaps in, and the bottom flap up, and glue together.

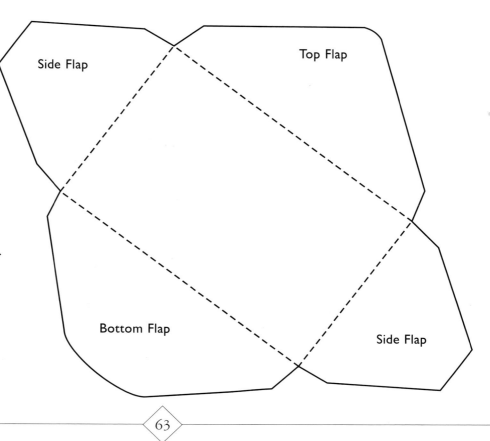

Side Flap

Top Flap

Bottom Flap

Side Flap

Index